The Entire Money Transformation: An Astute Method for Ensuring Financial Security

Brian T. Griner

All rights reserved. No part of this publication may be reproduced,
distributed, or transmitted in any form or by any means, including
photocopying, recording, or other electronic or mechanical methods,
without the prior written permission of the publisher, except in the case
of brief quotations embodied in critical reviews and certain other
noncommercial uses permitted by copyright law.
Copyright © Brian T. Griner, 2024.

Table of contents

[Chapter 1](#)
[Chapter 2](#)
[Chapter 3](#)
[Chapter 4](#)
[Chapter 5](#)
[Chapter 6](#)
[Chapter 7](#)
[Chapter 8](#)
[Chapter 9](#)
[Chapter 10](#)
[Chapter 11](#)
[Chapter 12](#)

Chapter 1

The Entire Money Transformation

Making use of positive thinking for money transformation

One of the most effective strategies for drawing prosperity and plenty into your life is positive thinking. You attract what you think to be your destiny—wealth and abundance—because your ideas and beliefs create your reality. You attract into your life what you concentrate on, according to the law of attraction, and the same is true with money. Thus, begin by altering your perspective and convictions toward money. Think that there is enough money in the world for everyone to have a portion since it is abundant. Imagine that you have a prosperous and financially independent existence. Pay attention to the benefits and chances that money might provide in your life.

Develop a Wealthy Attitude

It takes a wealth mentality to draw prosperity and money into your life. When it comes to building money, your thinking is your greatest advantage. Your financial success is determined by the thoughts, emotions, and actions you take around money. You need first alter your financial views to cultivate a wealth mentality. Think of money as a tool to help you design the life you want. Recognize that wealth is not a terrible thing, and possessing more of it won't make you a horrible person. Adopt a development mentality and keep an open mind to all the possibilities that lie ahead. Have faith in your abilities to generate riches.

A Money Magnet Mindset: What Is It?

Positivity toward money and prosperity is known as a "Money Magnet Mindset." It's the conviction that wealth is plentiful and that you should be entitled to it. Individuals who possess a Money Magnet Mindset see money as a tool to help them design the life they want and are not frightened of it. They are prepared to take chances to reach their objectives and are receptive to options that might help them get wealthier.

Conversely, those who have a scarcity mentality see money as a finite resource. They think that if someone else gets more, it implies there is less for them and that there isn't enough for everyone. They are mired in a cycle of need and scarcity and often fear taking chances.

What Makes Having a Money Magnet Mindset Vital?

Having a money-magnet mindset is crucial if you want to draw riches and prosperity into your life. Seeing possibilities to boost your income is more likely to occur when you have a good outlook on money. Additionally, you have a greater willingness to attempt new things and take chances to succeed financially.

A Money Magnet Mindset may also assist you in overcoming any bad habits and limiting ideas that could be preventing you from reaching your full potential. You are more likely to make decisions that advance your financial objectives when you think you deserve to live a prosperous life. Knowing that investing in yourself, your school and your profession will pay off in the long term will encourage you to do so more.

Form Sound Financial Practices

Creating sound financial habits is essential if you want to draw plenty and riches into your life. It's critical to practice smart and efficient money management. Make a budget and follow it as a starting point. Understand your spending and identify areas where you may make savings. Make it a habit to set aside a certain amount of money each month. Make sensible financial decisions and keep an open mind about potential new ventures. Try to stay out of debt as much as you can, and if you are in debt, make a strategy to pay it off quickly.

Act Now

The most important step in drawing richness and money into your life is taking action. You won't become wealthy with all the positive thinking, attitude, and sound financial practices until you put them into practice. Establish clear objectives first, then come up with a plan of action to achieve them. Take daily action to achieve your objectives by breaking them down into manageable chunks. Remain steadfast and constant, and don't give up at the slightest hint of difficulty. Acknowledge your errors and turn them into opportunities for growth and progress.

Embrace the Company of Successful People

Having prosperous individuals around you is a terrific way to draw prosperity and money into your life. Successful people have distinct habits and mindsets that have helped them succeed. You may take lessons from their experiences and use them in your own life by spending time with them. Make connections with like-minded individuals by attending conferences, seminars, and networking events. Be eager to learn and develop, and have an open mind to new concepts and viewpoints..

Chapter 2

debt fallacies

American debt has risen to $17 trillion as of June 2023, according to figures from the New York Federal Reserve Bank. This enormous amount covers a wide variety of debts, including credit card debt, vehicle loans, and the huge burden of mortgages, to name a few.

The top 7 misconceptions about debt are listed below.

1. A debt-ridden credit score is lower

Managing and navigating debt has a greater influence on your credit score than the sheer fact that you have debt. The way you handle your debt is extensively examined by creditors and credit bureaus. Your creditworthiness may be negatively impacted by persistently missing or making late payments, even if you are making conscientious efforts to pay off your mortgage.

In contrast, your credit score will increase if you continue to make regular payments on specific debts, like a mortgage or vehicle loan, and you retain those obligations. As a result, lenders will see that you are dedicated to efficiently decreasing your outstanding liabilities, which speaks well of your financial responsibility.

To put it simply, managing your obligations with caution and punctuality is more important than becoming debt-free. You may improve your credit score and become a more appealing customer to lenders by always paying your bills on time.

2. Bankruptcy will remain permanently on your credit record.

A person who finds themselves in a position where they are too indebted may find bankruptcy to be their only option because of the extreme difficulty of the situation. Bankruptcy is a scary proposition because of the potential long-term damage it might do to one's credit history in addition to its immediate consequences.

The fact that a bankruptcy will not remain on your credit record indefinitely should be understood, however. The effect on your creditworthiness is not permanent, even if it is unquestionably a tough choice with financial ramifications. Bankruptcy is usually totally deleted from your credit record after seven to 10 years of being included in it.

The procedure is difficult and might momentarily impair your financial situation, but it won't be a major barrier. You may slowly recover your creditworthiness and take steps toward a better financial future by practicing sensible money management and rebuilding.

3. Collection agencies don't handle small debts

It may seem unlikely that a $20 credit card debt from years ago can cause you to have headaches. Even small amounts of debt, however, might harm your credit score as they can be sent to collection agencies for resolution.

All outstanding obligations, no matter how little, must be aggressively sought out and paid off. Asking for a free copy of your credit report is a sensible move that will help you recognize and handle these obligations.

To further relieve the load of ongoing anxiety, it's worthwhile to investigate other methods for paying off your debts. Creating an organized repayment schedule or looking into debt consolidation alternatives may be necessary for this.

4. Making the Minimum Payment Is the Best Option

Examining your credit card account more closely may reveal a minimum payment requirement, leading you to believe that this is the only amount you must pay to be debt-free for the month. Making only the minimal payment exposes you to growing debt, however, and this is important to realize.

Actually, to keep the debt from ballooning into an untenable amount, it is advisable to pay off the whole amount each month. Your credit card issuer determines the interest rate that is applied to unpaid amounts, and it is usually much greater than the interest rates applied to other types of debt.

Regularly paying off the whole amount helps you develop appropriate financial habits in addition to avoiding the heavy interest rates. With this strategy, you can be confident that your credit card will continue to be a useful and affordable instrument instead of a constant source of debt.

5. Every Debt Is Negative Debt

There is such a thing as "good debt," which implies that having debt need not always indicate a dire financial state. Take your mortgage, for example, which may qualify as good debt. In the end, you get a physical asset in the form of real estate and can obtain housing as you progressively return the debt.

Likewise, since a student loan is an investment in your education, it may also be justifiedly seen as good debt. Your ability to make more money in the future might be greatly increased by this knowledge, too. Long-term benefits such as increased possibilities and future income might outweigh any debt that may be incurred now.

Good debt is, in essence, an investment in your long-term financial stability and progress. Ultimately, the benefits of having debt will be outweighed by the value assets or talents you acquire thanks to this strategic strategy.

Your Score Will Drop If You Check Your Credit Report

An important first step when applying for large loans such as mortgages or auto loans is evaluating your credit situation.

Fortunately, you may get a free copy of your credit report once a year from Equifax,

Experian, and TransUnion, the three main credit reporting agencies. Maintaining a close eye on your total debt and financial situation is made possible by this technique.

Notably, no effect of examining your credit report on your credit score. Furthermore, a large number of credit card companies provide their customers the option to see their credit ratings for free. You need to welcome this as a beneficial perk right away.

7. Your credit score will rise after canceling your credit card

It may surprise you to learn that canceling credit cards might negatively impact your credit score. This is because canceling a credit card shortens your credit history and reduces your available credit limit, both of which lead to a decrease in your credit score.

Keep just a few credit cards that you use regularly for longer periods; it would be a more responsible method. Throughout time, this method may help you become more creditworthy by allowing you to gradually improve your credit history.

Chapter 3
Myths about money

Myths and Misconceptions about Money
Almost anyone is willing to provide financial guidance. from your children as well as from leaders, educators, and parents! However, what are some common misunderstandings and fallacies regarding money from all these fields that we hold?

Let us try to dispel some of the myths and incomplete information you have been exposed to about debt management, investing, and saving. They can prevent you from achieving financial security.

Myth1: To save and invest, you must have a high-income
"Everything is excess, except money, so it needs to be managed well," said Lailah Giftie Akita. This quotation demonstrates

that the idea that you will begin saving money when you have more is only a way to run away from the truth.

You may accomplish your financial objectives by saving little sums over time, which can add up to a large sum. A portion of your salary should be put away for savings. By setting up standing orders on certain days, you may automate the procedure and save money with ease.

Myth 2: Only the Rich Can Invest Because It's Risky.
The only time investing is dangerous is when you don't know where or how to put your money. It's best to begin investing as soon as possible. You begin by taking advantage of low-risk assets such as a Roth IRA or a corporate 401(k) plan. After some time, even $20 a month will add up to a sizable sum. Compound interest is the eighth wonder of the universe, as stated by Einstein.

Because low-cost index funds provide wide market exposure, you may also look at them. Without costing you a single cent, robo-advisors may provide you with advice on what to think about. You may put away a portion of your income, regardless of how much you make, for investments.

Myth 3: All debt is not good debt
The world's ultra-wealthy would have you believe that taking on debt is the only way to increase your riches. Does this imply, therefore, that if you don't have a loan, you should be heading to the bank? Conversely, far away. Good debts, such as mortgages and school loans, enable you to use future income as leverage to increase your asset base.

When properly handled, debt may strengthen your financial position. A debt cycle might be avoided by avoiding consumer loans like high-interest credit cards and by having clear payback arrangements. All loans include some risk, therefore it's important to consider whether the risk is worthwhile.

Myth 4: You Can Put Off Saving for Later.
Assume you put off starting to save for ten years. If you save $50 a month in a monthly compound interest plan for ten years, you may forfeit almost $5,000 in returns. This may seem like a little sum, but if you save more, it could add up to a big sum.

Investing even a modest amount today can help you create a more secure financial future. Additionally, you may begin saving without having to pay off your house or college loans. The saying says, "The best time to start saving was yesterday; the second-best time is now."

Myth 5: Luck is the Only Factor in Financial Success

Even the world's richest individuals acknowledge that some chance plays a role in their success. But it just makes up a tiny portion of their achievements. Reaching your financial objectives requires knowledge, self-control, and wise financial choices.

To accumulate long-term wealth, chance is not enough. Financial literacy and action are the first steps in taking charge of your money. Investing in resources such as books, seminars, and forums that guide investing, spending, and saving may help establish a solid basis.

In summary,
The only way to become financially stable is to unlearn and then learn again. Certain things we take for granted may not be accurate, preventing us from reaching our objectives. Make wise judgments about investing, debt management, and saving by consulting trustworthy sources.

Chapter 4
obstacles for two months

The U.S. Bureau of Labor Statistics estimates that 20% of newly established companies fail within the first year. By their second year, over a third had failed, and within five years, half. The majority of these early losses are the result of misfires in one of the categories discussed below, however, some of these failures are attributable to unanticipated events.

Let's examine some of the typical challenges faced by aspiring business owners and how we resolve them.

1. Not planning: not knowing how to place the company
Your friends tell you, "I'd buy tons of your homemade cookies; they're great." You ought to launch a company. The notion

appeals greatly to you as an expert cookie maker who despises your present employment. You create an S-Corp, make purchases, design a website, and appoint one or more employees. After that, you bake, begin promoting, and wait. However, not many people purchase.

This example, in some form, is the standard narrative of the startup business owner. Many of us go on this path without using fundamental concepts of business. A shoemaker who decides to open a shoe store often overlooks this basic fact, as Michael E. Gerber notes in The E-Myth: running a company isn't actually about creating shoes.

To succeed, a large portion of the preliminary planning must cover The Five Ps of Marketing:

Product: What qualities, advantages, and primary appeal will persuade someone to purchase it?

Pricing: What is the appropriate charge? Crucially, how does the price affect the customer's perception of the product or service?

Placement: While your cookies are excellent, how will they be disseminated in terms of time and place?

Marketing: These days, with the growth of social media and other online platforms, spreading the word is much simpler. However, a successful marketing strategy depends on having a thorough grasp of the target market and identifying workable, quantifiable ways to contact them.

Positioning: The fit of the product in the market is this. What psychological, behavioral, and geographic characteristics of your primary target allow you to ascertain their needs and desires? For them, how do you stand out from the competition?

A new firm may fail if strategies are not planned or are not swiftly adjusted.

Most novice business owners just have a general idea of a handful of the aforementioned aspects or don't take into account all of them. Possibly the most significant problem I've seen and seen is the inability to properly position the product and grasp the market. We often attempt to please everyone and wind up disappointing no one. Alternatively, you choose a target market but it's the incorrect one, as I discovered with my first venture!

I believed that the target market for Fit2Go, my prepared meal service business, consisted of affluent professionals looking for a tasty and nutritious lunch. They would like the convenience of having freshly cooked gourmet meals delivered to their workplace, were busy, and could afford the price range. Regretfully, I learned that CEOs with greater salaries often go out to lunch.

Furthermore, the emphasis in the United States is on supper, but in my native Venezuela, lunch is a major event. I eventually identified the target market sweet spot—everyday workers who want supper alternatives that are hearty and flavorful—after much trial and error. It took me many years to come to that realization. However, a lot of entrepreneurs either release a product that is essentially unsuitable for the market or fail to address their targeting issue fast enough.

Distribution (placement) was yet another significant obstacle for me. Delivering freshly prepared meals throughout the full 6,137 square mile Miami-Dade region proved to be more difficult than I had anticipated. The cost was an additional challenge. Fit2Go's pricing had to be adjusted since I had expected it would appeal to a richer customer; this change had a big effect on cash flow and operations.

I could go on and on about the frequent blunders made by other young businesses, as well as my early planning mishaps. The primary error, however, is that you did not sufficiently study, comprehend, and organize the 5P marketing matrix. If we can't properly design a product and then price, market, and distribute it sensibly, then even the best company ideas will fail.

2. Creating the appropriate structure and staffing it appropriately
I recruited friends and relatives as soon as I launched my company.

"These are folks I know." They have a stake in my achievement. Additionally, when every dollar matters, they are affordable laborers.

Additionally, I employed strangers who had no experience in the industry and were underpaid. I thought it would be simple to force everyone to behave in the way I believed they ought to. Fit2Go lacked a well-thought-out organizational structure and distinct positions' responsibilities.

Everyone ended up taking on many roles and duties that overlapped.

All of them are traditional, basic recruiting errors.

When it comes to recruiting, a well-established, stable company has many more possibilities than a startup. Our substantial revenue enables us to hire competent, well-paid personnel. Additionally, we will have a clearer idea of who should be doing what by then. Even if they often lack the luxury of a consistent income, young business owners should nonetheless take great care in selecting their employees and understanding the interplay between various positions.

Understanding who you need and what each person will perform is crucial to having a clear framework. Even if a company may have all hands on deck, it is still crucial to guide individuals toward their areas of expertise rather than just throwing bodies at whatever is needed at the time. Roles and duties must be clearly stated.

Onboarding new workers who don't fit with the goals, culture, and fundamental values is another common source of difficulty. Sadly, a lot of business owners don't even attempt to specify their aims, culture, or beliefs, making it difficult to determine if a candidate fits in. I refer to those who consume the incorrect kind of energy as organizational "terrorists." Even if they could be competent, if they behave in a way that goes against your and the company's values, they can destroy the culture more quickly than you can create it.

Ultimately, a lot of us worry about the overhead associated with employing highly skilled and compensated workers, and some of us even see them as a challenge to our leadership.

The problem is straightforward when it comes to payment: "We can't afford them because money is tight." For $15,000 less, I can get this other individual who appears okay but may not be as wonderful. Although this impulse seems sense, a lot of seasoned company entrepreneurs alter their perspective. First, the applicant ends up saving or making far more money than the additional compensation if they are in line with the company's strategy and are highly talented and qualified for a critical function. Secondly, we do not intend to commit to a yearly pay. We are committed to the first ninety days of it so that we can determine whether or not they are a beneficial and excellent match.

The ego of a boss may often stand in the way of employing superstars. Some business owners believe that we don't need brilliant people in certain roles, or they may even see them as a danger. When I first began out, I employed individuals who I could control and direct. It took me a few years to realize how important it was to bring on team members who were not just very brilliant but also, in many cases, considerably more competent than I am.

Again, when we launch a new company, our alternatives are often restricted. The structure is changing, there is a lack of money, and new business owners want to feel in charge. However, the lesson is the same for established companies as well as startups: we should recruit the finest employees we can find and be prepared to pay a little bit more for them. "You (and your business) are the average of the people around you," to borrow an idiom. Superstar workers also significantly raise the likelihood of corporate success.

Chapter 5
save $10,000 quickly

How to Save $10,000 in a Year: For the majority,

A substantial sum of $10,000. That kind of money usually doesn't materialize without some kind of financial hardship. That becomes much more practical, however, if you consider $10,000 as saving just over $27 a day. Maintaining self-control and consistency in your financial matters is the key to overcoming any financial obstacle. You can turn a daunting $10,000 savings goal into a manageable financial accomplishment by following these eight steps.

Step 1: Understand why you do what you do

Without a specific goal in mind, saving money might seem unmotivating. Your progress may be hampered if you are tempted to take money out of your savings account. Prioritize long-term enjoyment above short-term satisfaction while planning for the future, particularly if you're saving $10,000. You may prioritize your savings strategy financially by understanding your "why."

You could be putting money aside to reload your emergency fund after using it to cover unforeseen costs. You may also choose to address credit card debt, save for your ideal trip, or get ready for your first house as your "why." For whatever reason, knowing why you are doing something may keep you inspired and focused on reaching your financial objective.

Step 2: Divide the objective into digestible portions.

It's normal to feel overwhelmed or demoralized by the enormity of a difficult savings target. Enormous objectives may also facilitate the simple detour into procrastination, which might lead to months of goal neglect. Nevertheless, it's still wiser to try to save money even if you fall short of your target or meet it at the eleventh hour. You may maintain focus on your goal throughout the year by breaking your target down into smaller, more doable pieces.

Financial short-term goals are a first step toward long-term objectives. You will need $833.33 in savings every month to attain $10,000 in a year. To put it even more simply, you'll need to set up $192.31 every week, or $27.40 per day. It's much simpler to measure your progress with these smaller portions since they're more realistic and easy to understand.

Step 3: Make your budget, or amend it.
Make a budget for college expenses if you don't already have one so you can track your spending. A budget aids in the long-term tracking of your earnings and outlays. Make sure to include all of your costs, both fixed and variable, when you first construct one.

The following are some typical budget areas to take into account: housing, utilities, entertainment, food, transportation, and insurance. You want to choose a certain category for your savings objective as well. Without requiring much work from you, setting aside a certain amount of money may help you keep your savings on track.

Keep in mind that making a budget does not require you to give up all of your pleasures. It involves striking a balance between your current needs and goals and conserving money for the future. You may reach your financial objectives and feel secure knowing where your money is going with a little preparation and self-control.

Step 4: Lower your costs
You may begin making cuts to your spending after reviewing your budget. For example, cutting down on meal delivery or streaming services might be necessary to achieve this. Alternatively, you might start cutting down on any costs that you are unable to remove or do not want to.

You may use some of these grocery store money-saving ideas, but you wouldn't give up food shopping altogether. The necessity for a new winter coat or interview attire would also not go unnoticed. But if you want to pay less for a high-quality item, you may go via secondhand stores. Perhaps you typically buy a few new books per year. Alternatively, you may get a library card, check out books from a friend, or read free digital books.

You may save money without sacrificing your quality of life by making substitutions for less expensive options. Furthermore, you only need to be resourceful to find several low-cost date ideas and economical solutions to ease your FOMO. Keep in mind that as long as it stays within your budget, it's OK to spend money on leisure.

Step5: Increase your income
Although reducing spending is a sensible approach to managing your money, there can come a time when you are unable to make more cost reductions. You may need to think about raising your income when you hit that ceiling. Fortunately, increasing your income while in college is rather easy.

You may think about getting a part-time job if you don't currently have one. In the same way, you may take on more hours if you're currently employed. You may include a flexible side hustle to your resume in cases when your schedule does not permit a typical career. Engaging in activities like pet sitting, yard work, or selling stuff you no longer need might increase your income.

Occasionally, however, you will be fortunate enough to not need to labor for your additional funds. Being creative and using your unexpected funds to your objective is a smart approach. "Found" money includes things like employment bonuses and birthday presents. Allocating your tax return to help you meet your savings target is also a wise use of the funds. Getting these additional dollars might make a big difference in your financial objectives.

Step 6: Manage your savings strategically
Paying yourself first is among the most straightforward methods for saving money. By using this technique, you may regard your savings as a payment that needs to be paid. Just like you would with a payment to your utility company or mobile phone provider, automate your savings every pay period or month.

You have two options for transferring money: automatically or manually from your checking to your savings account. Additionally, if you want to accelerate the growth of your savings, you might decide to place your money in a high-interest account. You may want to think about high-yield savings accounts or certificates of deposit (CDs) depending on when you want to reach your financial objective. Make sure you investigate which savings accounts best fit your requirements before you start.

Consider taking part in a savings challenge for a more entertaining approach to reaching your financial objectives. These little financial endeavors are fulfilling and inspiring. Furthermore, engaging in enjoyable money-saving activities may teach you new and efficient money-management techniques in addition to helping you save some cash.

Step 7: Evaluate and make changes

Consider how you have handled your finances throughout the year. Following any significant changes to your finances, you should also review the state of your budget. For instance, you may get a sizable inheritance or welcome a family member with four legs. You should modify your savings strategy by any changes in your financial circumstances, whether positive or negative.

You may use your phone to create a monthly reminder to check in on the status of your savings goal. Check what's and isn't functioning. You may change your spending plan or look for other methods to save money if you discover that you're not saving enough. You may put additional money toward your goal as your income rises, but be careful not to spend it all on impulse. You'll have more financial stability and independence in the future the more you save.

Step 8: Reward your accomplishments
No matter how much or how little you save, you should appreciate each accomplishment. Your financial achievements are worthy of celebration, whether you saved your first $1,000 or were able to follow your spending plan for a whole three months. You may stay

motivated on your financial path by promoting your good money habits.

Treating yourself to a special meal, organizing a picnic with friends, or organizing a family movie night are all wonderful ways to celebrate. If you would rather celebrate by yourself, you may read a new book, take a soothing bath, or go for a stroll in the outdoors. While it's good to be recognized for your achievements, it's just as crucial to avoid becoming broke in the process. Celebrate in a straightforward and fun way, and don't allow them to overshadow the accomplishments you've already done.

Ideally, you will have a nice $10,000 nestled into your bank account a year after following these eight instructions. This objective may be financially attained with the correct money attitude. But if you make a mistake or miss a savings goal, try not to be too harsh on yourself. Failures are a natural part of life, and they happen to everyone. Rather, concentrate on regaining your direction and continuing forth. You'll quickly meet your $10,000 savings target if you're committed and persistent.

Chapter 6

The domino effect of debt

Is the four-letter word that begins with D and finishes with T haunting you? Then, it's essential to launch an offensive and implement a reliable debt repayment strategy. There are several strategies for getting rid of debt. The Debt Snowball Method, which consists of five steps, is widely used. Let's examine this debt-busting method that might completely change your financial situation.

The Debt Snowball Method's Operation

One well-liked debt payback technique that might assist you in getting out of debt and achieving financial independence is the Debt Snowball Method. Paying off the lowest debt first and making minimal payments on other obligations entails allocating debts according to their amounts.

A snowball effect is produced, speeding up debt payments as the money freed up from one loan is carried over to the next.

The Debt Snowball Method's primary idea is to psychologically motivate people by emphasizing little victories. People feel a feeling of success and progress when they pay off the lowest debt first, and this motivates them to keep going with their debt-reduction path. This approach works especially well for those who need more encouragement to stick to their debt payback schedule.

It is essential to remember that the Debt Snowball Method does not rank loans according to their interest rates. Although some financial experts contend that paying off high-interest loans first might result in longer-term financial savings, the Debt Snowball Method emphasizes the emotional benefits of debt repayment and builds momentum by concentrating on paying off lesser obligations first.

Orient Yourself to Succeed
Like most things in life, this debt-busting strategy won't work unless you have a plan of attack. This necessitates the establishment of a personal budget so that you are aware of the precise amount you can afford to allocate to debt repayment. Together with creating a repayment plan, you must also compile a list of all of your debts, amounts, interest rates, and minimum monthly payments. We'll walk you through how to divide this activity into manageable chunks below.

Determine Your Debt. And by all, we mean all.
Making a thorough inventory of all of your obligations is a prerequisite for using the Debt Snowball Method. Credit card balances, department or specialty shops, Affirm, AfterPay, personal loans, school

loans, etc. are all included in this. The one exception is that, if you have a mortgage, you should leave it off. Make sure to mention each debt's interest rate, minimum monthly payment, and outstanding amount.

You may get a good picture of your whole financial status by making a list of your debts. It enables you to appropriately prioritize your bills and view the wider picture. You can simply monitor your progress and maintain organization throughout your debt payback journey by keeping a thorough inventory of all of your debt.

Sort them by height, small to tall.
Sorting your debts by balance, from lowest to greatest, is the next step once you have made a list of them. This entails listing your debts according to their outstanding sums in increasing order. On the list, the debt with the lowest amount will be at the top and the highest amount at the bottom.

A key component of the Debt Snowball Method is sorting your debts by balance, which establishes the sequence in which you will pay them off. Commencing with the least amount of debt allows you to reap immediate benefits and provide impetus for your debt settlement process. You may maintain your motivation and attention throughout the procedure by following this sequence.

Begin Small
The Debt Snowball Method's main tenet is to settle the lowest debt first while paying the required minimum payments on other obligations. putting more money toward the lowest debt until it is settled in full. The money that was previously allotted for the payment of the lowest debt is transferred to the next smallest obligation on your list after it has been paid off.

You ask, what more money? We are talking about the "extra" cash that is included in your operating budget. This indicates that they are not used for other purposes, such as paying for housing, food, utilities, health insurance, or other necessities of daily living. Usually, you may find them by going over a few months' worth of costs and finding areas where you can reduce wasteful spending. This includes cash spent on dining out, impulsive buys, streaming subscriptions, and the all-time favorite, the Starbucks run, which is a budget killer. Spending less on frivolous items allows you to put that additional cash toward paying off debt.

Create Energy
By using this strategy to pay off each obligation, you generate a snowball effect that gains momentum and quickens the payback of your debt. By rolling over the money from the paid-off obligation to the next largest loan on your list, you may

accelerate the payment timeline and increase the amount available for repayment. As you go forward with your debt repayment plan, you'll notice that your motivation to pay off your obligations and reach financial independence increases.

This is an illustration of how the Debt Snowball technique may seem in day-to-day activities. You have two credit cards, $5,000 (at 18.9% APR) and $7,500 (at 25.99% APR), plus a $300 medical bill that you are not paying interest on. In this case, your priority would be to settle the medical expense. Why? Considering that the debt has the lowest balance. Although it may seem counterintuitive, if you start your debt-elimination path with victories, you'll be more inclined to remain with it.

Chapter 7
Empathy Reserve

Set aside for the inevitable rainy day, an emergency fund is a specific savings account designed to meet unforeseen expenses that may arise over time. Anything from unforeseen auto repairs to unforeseen medical costs may be covered by this fund.

Even while most Americans recognize the need to have an emergency fund, many are unsure of how much money they truly need to save or where to begin. Here's everything you need to know about emergency savings accounts and how to begin setting one up.

Why should you have an emergency fund?
Nobody ever plans for an emergency. Unexpected events often arise and may rapidly turn into financial obligations, whether it's chipping a tooth at lunch or

needing to replace a water heater that unexpectedly breaks.

You are partially equipped to handle life's financial curveballs if you have an emergency fund in place. You are now ahead of a significant number of households: 37% of Americans would not be able to pay an unforeseen $400 bill without using credit cards or loans, according to Federal Reserve statistics from 2022. This figure jumps to 43% among parents in America.

Common issues like the following are some costs that might cost you at least $400:

Emergencies related to health or dentistry.
vehicle maintenance.
house fixes.
A big electricity or tax bill.
A sudden loss of consistent income or the necessity for a new $9,000 HVAC system in the heat of July are two scenarios that might result in far higher costs. In these cases,

you'll probably require a loan or credit card. However, most little shocks may be avoided without causing financial hardship if you have a sizable emergency fund in place.

What much should I have in my emergency fund?
In an emergency fund, you should ideally have three to six months' worth of costs saved. if it won't happen quickly, you can achieve this goal, even if it may seem overwhelming if you're just now beginning to save for a rainy day.

To cover unforeseen costs, start by trying to save at least $500 to $1,000. Better still, if you can fulfill your other savings targets and manage to save more than that.

As nothing is better than anything, make a short-term goal for yourself based on your spending patterns and present budget. Set a more ambitious objective and begin working toward it after you've started to save emergency funds. After a while, you'll build up an emergency fund that will help you out in case your employer dismisses you or your automobile requires new brake linings.

My emergency fund: where should I put it?
Your emergency money is most effectively placed in:

a specific account that is unrelated to your everyday savings, meaning you won't access it.
An account that is easily accessed in an emergency.
an account that yields the highest interest rate feasible.
A high-yield savings account (HYSA) has all of these characteristics. When your money is sitting but still liquid, you may optimize the interest you receive on your balance with a HYSA. If you don't run into any unforeseen costs, your interest will only increase. If you do, you won't face any fees or difficulties and may easily get the money you want.

Maybe the only savings account your current bank offers is a standard one. That is an option, particularly if you would like to have all of your accounts maintained by the same financial institution so that simple transfers between savings and checking accounts and total balance monitoring are made possible. Alternatively, if you save a particular amount, you can be eligible for additional perks like an improved checking account.

However, excessive access to funds is a problem for some individuals. If there is just a mental barrier separating your emergency cash from your normal savings account, you may be tempted to cross it and splurge.

Your emergency money should thus be left alone, just like the cheese. Additionally, you may often get the best interest rates with online-only banks, even if your physical bank provides a HYSA. Look around; you'll thank me for it.

How to accumulate funds for emergencies
Each person has a somewhat distinct savings plan, which is based on things like their present spending plan, monthly savings target, and amount of savings already in place. Here are some pointers to get you started if you want to create an emergency fund from scratch.

Establish a budget. Without a budget, it's difficult to achieve any financial objective. Take some time to create one for yourself, using the 50/30/20 rule (needs, 30% desires, 20% savings) or just shoving cash into an envelope for each distinct monthly bill. Make sure you include donations as a separate line item for your emergency fund.
Set incremental objectives. Although having enough money saved for six months or more is the ideal emergency fund, this might be challenging for families who are living

paycheck to paycheck. If you fit this description, start with smaller, more manageable objectives and save the larger ones for later. As an example, set a $500 savings target at first, then increase it to $1,000 (i.e., a total of $1,500 saved).

Make the procedure automatic. Savings initiatives that are impervious to sabotage tend to be the most effective. You remove the possibility of forgetting to save one month or convincing yourself not to save during hard times by automating your savings. Just after paycheck, set up an automated transfer from savings to emergency fund.

Look for methods to increase the scale of your work. Do you want to sell anything on Facebook Marketplace? Discover forty concealed in the coat pocket from last winter? Put any additional money you get as a bonus into your emergency fund. You won't experience any pinching as you accelerate toward your objective.

Make money with the money you have. You may make sure that your money grows as much as possible by selecting the greatest interest rate on your savings. Seek a HYSA that accumulates interest every day rather than only once a month.

Out of mind, out of sight. Like most individuals, you can feel pressured to take money out of savings when a significant purchase comes along. Maintain a separate account only for your emergency fund. In this manner, raiding is an active decision.

Put extra money aside. It is impossible to have too much savings. Aim higher after your emergency fund targets have been reached. Look at alternative savings accounts that can benefit from your work after you've saved enough money for six months' worth of expenditures, such as a college or retirement fund.

Timestamp: Make accumulating emergency savings your priority.

To avoid having to depend on loans, credit cards, or other consumer debt when life occurs, an emergency fund is a safety net meant to shield you and your family from unforeseen expenditures. Establishing an emergency fund should be among your first financial objectives. It will provide you with the assurance that you are prepared for everything from unexpected job loss to automobile difficulties to medical emergencies.

Chapter 8
optimize your retirement fund allocation

After all, a lot of your costs will persist even after you leave your first job behind. You still have regular expenses to pay in addition to unforeseen expenses that can come as a surprise. Do not fret. You may make the most of your next chapter if you optimize your retirement funds.

Here are six ways that may assist with retirement planning, including how much to save, what percentage of income to put toward retirement, and how to replace your pay once you reach that milestone:

Assume accountability for your retirement.
It's unlikely that our parents considered retirement savings amounts when they were just starting. Pensions were more widespread in the past, especially in the

professions of education and healthcare. Because of this, many workers were almost assured a lifelong income in retirement, usually determined by their annual wage and years of service.

Pensions are less frequent these days, however. For employees, this implies that because you are responsible for your retirement, it is prudent to plan and save as much as possible, monitor your assets, and determine how to turn your savings into a reliable source of income in retirement.

2. Begin using a diverse retirement strategy to safeguard your income.
To lessen your exposure to market risks while you're preparing for retirement, it's critical to diversify your assets among many investment kinds. The same goes for receiving income in retirement: Putting up an income plan with funds from several sources may help you manage the risks

associated with retirement, both anticipated and unforeseen.

One may generate varied retirement income in a variety of ways. You may better safeguard your income from retirement-related risks by combining at least some of the sources shown in the accompanying chart.

Certain sources of income—such as Social Security, pensions, and, if qualified, fixed annuities—are impervious to market fluctuations and provide a steady stream of income that one cannot outlive. Stocks, mutual funds, and variable annuities are examples of investments with growth potential that may increase in value while also helping to keep up with inflation.

When circumstances change, the upward movement of one asset class may help balance the negative movement of another if your long-term portfolio contains a variety of asset classes.

3. Establish a lifelong income stream with room to expand.

Annuities are growing more and more popular as a source of lifelong guaranteed income as pensions become obsolete and Social Security only partially replaces pre-retirement salaries. You may have both the possibility for ongoing development and a consistent, dependable income stream for the rest of your life with a diversified retirement plan that incorporates lifetime income from both fixed and variable annuities.

An income stream with growth potential that might help keep up with inflation is provided by variable annuities. Although the precise amounts of your income stream are guaranteed for life, they will fluctuate depending on how well the underlying assets perform. The hazards of investing in securities apply to your money and might include principal loss. For life or a certain length of time, fixed annuities guarantee a set sum. While this may help protect your income from market risk, your guaranteed income flow is not impacted by market volatility, so it may not keep up with inflation.

Fixed and variable annuities that might support your requirements for varied retirement income and manage potential hazards are something your company could provide. Employer retirement programs often provide annuities at a cheaper cost than retail annuities.

4. Have enough money saved to purchase the pair

A common question is what proportion of income should be set aside for retirement. If your workplace plan offers a match, you should aim to save a minimum amount to get that match from your company. If not, you're losing out on free money.

For instance, your company may match up to 6% of your entire pay, or one dollar for every $1 you save. A little percentage point or two lost on the match may have a significant impact on your overall savings when determining how much to contribute.

5. Observe the impact a small amount of money may have.
Take this into consideration if you believe you are unable to pay to your employer's plan: Raising your contributions to a retirement plan might help reduce your total taxed income.

For instance, your salary would be $75 less if you start contributing $100 each week and make $50,000 per year (assuming you are in the 25% federal tax rate).

Additionally, if you contribute any money to a workplace plan and have your company match it, you will at least partially reap the benefits of your potential.

6. Seek for other retirement savings options. To optimize retirement savings and income for your future, you must begin saving as soon as possible, regardless of the amount of money you can set aside.

Chapter 9
financing for colleges

You have special chances for college preparation as a company owner. It could be beneficial for you to transfer assets or income to your kid, who is usually at a lower tax rate if you are in a high tax bracket. Generally speaking, you may use one of the following methods to transfer company revenue to your child:

Give your youngster equity in the firm.
Give your youngster a stake in a S company or partnership.
Set up a gift-leaseback arrangement with your kid.
Put your kid on the payroll of the business.
All of these tactics have one thing in common: they all aim to take advantage of reduced tax rates by moving firm assets or revenue to a lower tax band.

1. Present shares in the firm

If you want to give your child's valued business stock and let them sell it, you may be able to move the subsequent capital gain into a lower tax rate if you intend to sell the shares to pay for college. Your kid may then use the money from the sale to cover their education costs. But there could be some compromises.

Firstly, your tax savings may be limited by the child tax. A child's unearned income above a specific amount ($2,300 in 2022) is subject to parent income tax rates under the kiddie tax regulations. Children under the age of eighteen and full-time college students under the age of twenty-four who earn less than half of their support are often subject to the kiddie tax.

Second, if the stock is sold for more than the yearly gift tax exclusion ($16,000 for solo gifts and $30,000 for combined gifts in 2022), this technique can have gift tax ramifications.

Third, this tactic might result in a smaller financial assistance package for your kid. When calculating financial assistance, kid assets—whether they be real stock shares or savings account earnings from a sale—are given a higher weight than parent assets under the federal government's approach. It is thus advised by most college counselors that your kid have minimal assets registered in his or her name on the completion of the financial assistance application.

Fourth, finding a market for your tightly held company's shares may be challenging. The IRS may consider a prearranged sale to a different family member to be a fraudulent transaction. However, in the unlikely event that the stock is purchased by a non-member of your family or close acquaintances, your family can wind up co-owning the company with an unknown individual. When selling to a close relative, get legal or tax guidance to avoid the IRS seeing the transaction as fraudulent.

2. Transfer an interest in an S corporation or partnership.

You may be able to transfer money to your kid by giving them an ownership stake in the firm if your company is taxed as an S corporation or partnership. Your kid may accrue distributions of business revenue (unearned income) to pay for college after you have given them an interest in the company. However, as previously mentioned in the preceding section, the kiddie tax may restrict your tax savings and this technique may diminish your child's financial assistance award.

Example(s): Anne is the proprietor of a temp agency that is organized as a S company. The company is worth $400,000.

Anne is the only shareholder and her tax rate is the highest. Anne wants to set up a college fund for her eight-year-old son, Noah. For ten years, Anne gives Noah $16,000 worth of nonvoting shares each year. By keeping her donations within the yearly gift tax exclusion level, Anne will be able to avoid paying federal gift tax. Noah will get dividends on the S company shares in the early years, which he may use to save for education. However, because of the child tax regulations, Noah's tax savings will also be restricted.

On the other hand, the IRS has regulations controlling who may own stock in a company that is recognized as an S corporation for taxation reasons. To ensure that adding your kid as a shareholder to your S company won't affect the business's tax status, speak with a tax expert or attorney. Furthermore, for your kid to be eligible to participate in a partnership, they must be able to sign a partnership agreement in your state. Generally speaking, your kid has to have become an adult or acted via a legally appointed trustee, conservator, or guardian. Speak with a tax expert or lawyer who is knowledgeable about your state's legislation.

Furthermore, there are expenses related to this approach. A partnership agreement has to be drafted by an attorney. Tax returns and documents need to be submitted. Evaluations have to be done. The proper titling documents must be prepared, and transfers must be recorded. Moreover, trust documentation has to be created if a trust is advised. Take these costs into account when calculating your possible tax savings. A corporate attorney is required to manage stock transfers and, if necessary, the issuing of nonvoting shares in the case of a S company.

3. Set up a transaction for gift-leaseback.

In a gift leaseback, one person transfers ownership of the property to another, who then leases it back. The main topic of discussion here is how a parent or company owner might lower the family's total federal income tax obligation by transferring an asset to a kid via a gift-leaseback agreement.

Giving a sizable commercial asset (such as a building, land, or equipment) to your kid directly or to an irrevocable trust for their benefit is the standard approach in a gift-leaseback deal. When parents feel uneasy giving a significant asset to their kids directly, they often establish trust. To lease the asset back, you then sign a fair market lease with your kid or the trust. The leasing payments go toward your child's income, and you may write them off as a business expenditure.

Example(s): Dr. Robinson owns the medical facility where he practices and has a prosperous medical practice. He pays taxes in a high bracket. He would want to establish a college fund for his little kid. For his child's benefit, Dr. Robinson may give the building to an irreversible trust. The building might then be leased back to him at a reasonable market rate by the trust. These funds "flow-through" to the kid from the trust.

The primary advantage of a gift-leaseback arrangement between a parent and kid is that the parent may transfer money to their child—who is most likely in a lower income tax bracket—in the form of lease payments. The youngster may then utilize this money to fund their college education, along with the tax savings that follow. Parents may also write off the lease payments as a business expenditure, provided that the gift-leaseback arrangement is correctly set up.

The primary disadvantage of a gift leaseback is that, depending on the value of the asset being presented to your kid, you, the giver, may have to pay gift tax. Additionally, child assets are given greater weight than parent assets when it comes to financial assistance. You will not be subject to federal gift tax if the value of the gift is less than the annual gift tax exclusion level, which in 2022 is $16,000 for solo gifts and $32,000 for combined gifts. You can be responsible for gift tax if the gift exceeds this amount, but your relevant exclusion amount may be used to reduce your liability.

Remember that the IRS closely monitors gift-leaseback transactions to ascertain if they are legitimate, that is, based on current rental rates and market values. This is particularly valid for business dealings involving family members, such as parents and children. This implies that the fair market value of the item being donated as well as the appropriate rental amount for that asset should be ascertained by a trained independent assessor. A formal lease agreement with regular provisions for that kind of property should also be included. A penalty clause for violations of the lease, such as an explicit penalty for late lease payments, needs to be included in the agreement. The IRS interprets these characteristics as proof that the gift-leaseback arrangement is legitimate.

If you transfer the wealth to a trust rather than to your kid directly, the trustee of the trust ought to be unrelated to you and your family. Additionally, parents should refrain from designating their accountant or lawyer as the trustee. Ideally, the trustee—such as a bank or an independent fiduciary—should be impartial. Furthermore, if a trust is utilized, it should not include a clause that gives you the right to reclaim the property at a later date (also known as a reversionary interest). The IRS may not see this agreement as a genuine gift if it has such a clause, in which case the leasing payments would not be deducted.

Additionally, there are some tax ramifications to consider. As previously stated, the parent may completely deduct the lease payments as an ordinary and necessary business cost (if the leased item is used in the parent's trade or company) if the gift-leaseback is correctly structured. The kid may be able to deduct part of the lease income from the item they have bought by claiming depreciation deductions, but they still have to record the lease payments as income. Finally, as was previously mentioned, depending on the value of the item being donated, gift tax may be owed. For assistance in putting a gift leaseback into effect or for further information, speak with a tax expert or attorney.

4. Enroll your youngster in the business payroll

By adding your kid to your company's payroll, you may be able to move your income into a lower tax rate. In the family company, your kid may work and earn a weekly wage while saving money for college.

Example(s): Dan is in the highest tax bracket and runs a tightly-held company. Molly, his daughter, is hired by him to work in the family company. She is paid every week, just like other workers. She makes $180 a week working 15 hours a week at $12 an hour. After fifty weeks, Molly receives $9,000. Molly will have more money available to spend toward education since she is at a lower tax rate than if Dan had earned the $9,000.

To find out what age and how many hours your kid may work lawfully, check your state's child labor regulations. Additionally, be cautious that the IRS can consider any remuneration you provide your kid beyond what is considered a fair amount to be a gift.

There are several advantages to this tactic. First off, because this money is earned rather than unearned, it is exempt from the kiddie tax. Second, because your kid is making their own money, gift tax is not applicable. Third, because he or she will have received money, your kid will be qualified to start an IRA. Fourth, if a kid under the age of 18 works for his or her parents in a trade or company that is a sole proprietorship or a partnership in which each partner is a parent of the child, the child will not be required to pay Social Security or Medicare taxes. Lastly, your youngster may pick up some transferrable skills and get real-world job experience by working in a family firm.

But, as was previously said, if your kid is applying for financial help, this tactic may lessen their reward since the federal government's financial aid methodology gives more weight to the assets of the child than to the assets of the parent. One way to help your kid with financial assistance is to have them form an IRA, because neither the federal government nor universities consider an IRA as an asset if your child has saved a significant amount of money working at the family company. Also, there is no early distribution penalty on withdrawals from an IRA utilized for educational costs.

Chapter 10

settle the mortgage on your house

Ways to pay off your mortgage stress-free

While monthly installments may seem overwhelming, if you follow these suggestions, you'll be debt-free in no time.
New homeowners suffer from a peculiar ailment that causes them to scream and emit unusual squealing noises. The phenomenon known as the "first-time-seeing-the-mortgage-bill" syndrome is real, and let's face it—thinking about having to pay $1,400+ a month for the next 25 years is scary.

However, remain composed; there are solutions available:

First, a reasonable assessment of the monthly payback costs

Since four-room HDB flats are among the most frequent forms of housing in Singapore, we will use them as our example.

The cost is around $430,000 on average. 75% of the flat's purchase price or value, whichever is smaller, may be covered by a bank home loan; however, if you purchase from HDB, the bank will often accept HDB's pricing as a reasonable valuation.

When subsidies like the CPF Housing Grant are taken into account, the actual cost will be lower. Visit the HDB website to find out what grants you qualify for.

By this, you are taking out a $322,500 loan.

At the time of writing, the interest rate is around 2% annually, with a maximum loan length of 25 years. This equates to a monthly loan repayment of around $1,410 over the next 25 years.

Alright, don't worry. There are solutions for handling this:

Recognize that you may make repayments with cash or CPF.

Try to borrow less.

Recall that you have up to $20,000 available in your CPF OA.

Think about accepting a different borrower.

When choosing a house, aim for the 30% target.

To maintain a low-interest rate, think about refinancing every few years.

1. Recognize that you may make repayments using cash or CPF.

Your house loan may be repaid using your CPF Ordinary Account (CPF OA) rather than having to be paid back in cash. This holds whether you utilize a bank loan or an HDB loan.

(In case you were wondering, the answer is that you may use CPF to pay for debts secured by private property).

You are only able to utilize so much CPF, however. With a bank loan, you may only utilize up to 120% of your home's Valuation Limit (VL); above that, you will have to make cash payments to repay the loan. Additionally, when you sell the residence, you'll have to refund the CPF funds that were utilized at a 2.5% interest rate.

With this knowledge, you may decide whether to pay with cash or CPF.

You may choose to use your CPF (which you are required to contribute to anyway) to make payments if you are presently on a limited budget. You'll have extra money after this for unforeseen costs or everyday spending.

Alternatively, you may decide to pay with cash provided your funds are in order. This will enable you to more effectively save for retirement with your CPF funds (you may even move any unused funds from your CPF OA into your CPF Special Account to get a higher guaranteed interest rate).

Consult a knowledgeable financial adviser to determine which is most appropriate for you.

The value or price of the property is simply subtracted to get the VL.

2. Try to borrow less money.
If you purchase your apartment with a bank loan, you may pay 75% of the cost with the

loan (see above), 20% with cash or CPF, and only 5% with actual cash.

By using the $430,000 apartment mentioned above as an example, you may borrow $322,500, pay $86,000 more out of CPF OA, and only need to pay $21,500 in cash.

If you split this with your spouse, for example, it may be extremely inexpensive for some of you. If you were to split 50/50, for instance, you would both just need to withdraw $43,000 from your separate CPF accounts and $10,750 in cash.

What happens, therefore, if you discover that you have more than enough money for the down payment? Well, you may reduce your mortgage repayment burden by taking on less debt.

Say, for instance, that you choose to accept 70% financing rather than the whole amount (a loan of $301,000 for a $430,000 apartment). Instead of almost $1,410 each month, the repayments now total roughly $1,275.

This leaves you with an additional $135 each month that you may use for savings, leisure, etc. Even when spread out over a lengthy term like a 25-year loan, it's not a little sum.

Don't let the large numbers scare you. To put that into perspective, five years before you purchase a home, you might get that amount by just saving $180 a month.

3. As a safety precaution, leave $20,000 in your CPF OA.
Think about leaving up to $20,000 in your CPF OA when utilizing it for the down payment. While saving the whole $20,000 is not necessary, you should think about saving at least six months' worth of the

mortgage ($8,460 in our four-room apartment).

In the event of a layoff, incapacity to work, etc., this guarantees you can pay the mortgage back while you heal. In the worst situation, you have six months to downsize and sell your apartment.

4. Contemplate accepting a different borrower.
If money is very tight, consider taking on another borrower, such as a parent (if they don't have any other outstanding house loans), working children, or a sibling.

They must sign the deed for them to be considered a co-owner; you cannot be a borrower alone. But in tight circumstances, one more donor might help make the mortgage manageable.

However, make sure the co-borrower is someone you get along with and trust;

otherwise, there may be disagreements on the road, such as if you want to sell the home but they won't allow you.

5. When choosing a house, aim for the 30% threshold.
To prohibit you from taking out a loan if the repayments surpass 35% of your monthly family income, HDB currently employs a Mortgage Servicing Ratio (MSR). Your monthly loan payments cannot exceed $2,800 if, for example, your family income is $8,000 per month.

To make things simpler for you and your mortgage, we advise you to limit it to 30% (i.e. no more than $2,400 every month). You still have 70% of your income left over, which you may use for retirement savings and long-term investments.

This is particularly crucial to remember when purchasing private residences. Private properties are governed by the Total Debt Servicing Ratio (TDSR) as opposed to the MSR. Since it permits your overall debt (credit cards, personal loans, etc.) to exceed 60% of your monthly income, the TDSR is more lenient.

However, it would be reckless to devote 60% of your monthly income to debt repayment; you run the risk of living paycheck to paycheck or having nothing saved for the future.

Aim to maintain a debt-to-income ratio of 30% or below. This is not a game to get the highest possible score.

Recall that interest rates on real estate loans are subject to fluctuation; for instance, if you have a SIBOR loan, your rate will likely increase every four years or more. The good news is that the interest rate on your CPF account, or savings account, is often greater than the interest rate on your house loan.

For instance, even though house loans typically have an annual growth rate of 2%, your CPF OA increases at a rate of 2.5%. You may earn interest of up to 3.8% on your savings account, such as a DBS multiplier account. When your money grows more quickly than your debt, that's always a positive thing.

The most crucial guideline is to begin modestly.
Recall that you may always sell and move up to a larger house in the future. Avoid taking on more debt than you can manage when it comes to your first mortgage. Try to keep your home's overall cost less than five times your yearly family income as much as you can. If you follow through on that, getting a mortgage should be easy.

102

Chapter 11
life after mortgage repayment

What to do after your mortgage is paid off
Making the most of any potential new financial prospects may depend on your ability to navigate the phases that come following paying off your mortgage. Here are some actions that may be useful:

1. Honoring the accomplishment
It's worth celebrating when your mortgage is paid off. Spending time with loved ones and friends to acknowledge this noteworthy achievement. A stimulating method to start this new and exciting phase of your life may be to acknowledge all the hard work you put into your mortgage.

2. Taking care of your future payments and escrow amount
It might be useful to find out how much money is left in your escrow account. You

will normally be in charge of paying future property taxes and homeowner's insurance once your mortgage is paid off. Creating a proactive strategy to handle these payments on your own may assist in maintaining order.

3. Keeping your local tax authorities and insurance provider informed
Make sure your local taxation authority and homeowner's insurance provider are informed of the change in your property's lien status after paying off your mortgage. The homeowner is usually responsible for this.

4. Changing your spending plan and stopping automated mortgage payments
If you have automated mortgage payments set up with your bank, you may wish to cancel them and adjust your budget to account for the difference in your spending. This might be a great chance to reallocate

money for investments, savings, or other financial objectives.

5. Rearranging documents and evaluating your insurance requirements
It's typically a good idea to keep any mortgage-related paperwork neatly filed in your files for future use. Now can be a good time to review your insurance requirements to make sure your coverage still fits your needs and budget.

advantages of loan repayment
Your financial status may improve as a result of paying off your mortgage, giving you more flexibility in how you spend your money. Let's look at a few particular benefits that might accompany becoming mortgage-free:

monetary adaptability
With the mortgage payment removed from the equation, you may be able to investigate other investing opportunities, think about

creating a retirement fund, or just take some well-earned time off.

Enhanced mental tranquility
For many people, having your mortgage paid off might result in more mental tranquility. You could feel more stable and secure knowing that your house is paid for in full, which might give you more energy and intensity to devote to other areas of your life.

Life after a mortgage: What comes next?
After paying off your mortgage, you may be wondering how to take full advantage of the opportunities that now present themselves. You now have the chance to consider fresh approaches and objectives. Let's examine some actions to think about doing on your post-mortgage path.

Reevaluate your financial objectives and budget.

Now that your mortgage has been paid off, it's a great moment to review your financial objectives and budget. Since you originally took out your mortgage, you may have developed new priorities or goals. You may be able to reallocate your resources to better match your changing objectives and aspirations by assessing your existing financial condition.

Put your attention on house upkeep and upgrades.
Now that you have some additional money, you could think about making repairs and upgrades to your house. Your living area may be made more delightful with regular maintenance and improvements. If you decide to sell or rent out your house in the future, these initiatives could also help you preserve or raise its value.

Put money into your future.
After a mortgage, you have the chance to make investments in your future. Some

homeowners may decide to buy a second house, holiday property, or investment property with their newly found financial freedom. These kinds of endeavors may open up new revenue sources and aid in your long-term wealth accumulation. Seek expert guidance from a financial adviser.

In conclusion, living after the payoff of your mortgage has the potential to be exciting. Reaching this goal creates a lot of possibilities, including the possibility of increased financial security and even personal development. Building a solid foundation for future success may be achieved by embracing your newly acquired financial independence and making proactive plans.

Chapter 12
produce enormous riches

Experts say that the best methods to make money are via digital marketing, lease rental discounts, Airbnb rentals, stock investments, and lease rentals. How can I become money quickly? Here are some investment choices for you to consider if you want to develop your extra money and eventually become wealthy:

1) Stock Investing
Stock investments have the potential to be an effective long-term wealth-growth strategy. Investing in shares of a business allows you to profit from its expansion and success while also becoming a part owner.

For example, owing to Amazon's exponential growth, a $1,000 investment in the business in 2001 would have grown to almost $1 million by 2021.

2) Rental Houses

Possessing and leasing homestay houses, via services like Airbnb, may provide a substantial revenue stream. For instance, a house in a well-liked tourist area with a prime location might bring in a sizable profit.

In addition to perhaps allowing for personal usage during other seasons, a house in a ski resort location may provide significant rental revenue during the winter.

3) Discounting on Lease Rentals

Banks and other financial institutions make loans secured by future rental revenue under a financial instrument known as Lease Rental Discounting (LRD). An owner of commercial real estate, for instance, may be eligible for an LRD loan based on the anticipated rental revenue from tenants.

You may leverage your current assets by using this to finance further investments or company development.

4) Internet-based advertising
Proficiency in digital marketing may open doors to a profitable profession or company in the modern day. For example, firms may boost their online exposure and profitability by launching a digital marketing agency and providing services like search engine optimization (SEO), pay-per-click (PPC) advertising, and social media marketing.

By offering their customers their skills in digital marketing, successful companies such as Neil Patel Digital have seen exponential growth.

5) Set Amount Objectives
Establishing definite financial objectives is an essential first step in building money. For

example, you may create an investing and savings strategy that is specifically designed to help you reach your retirement goals comfortably.

Regular contributions to retirement accounts, such as an IRA or 401(k), allow you to benefit from compound interest and perhaps accumulate a sizeable nest egg for retirement.

6) Eliminate Your Debt
When trying to achieve financial security, paying off high-interest debt needs to be your first focus. Paying off credit card debt, for example, may provide an 18% return on investment if the loan has an annual interest rate of 18%. Paying off debt quickly allows you to have more money for investments and savings.

As an example, let's say you owe $10,000 on credit cards, with an interest rate of 18%. You may save around $2,000 in interest payments by paying off the loan in about 24 months if you make regular monthly payments of $500.

7) Make a Pillow

Having an emergency fund in place can help you pay for unforeseen costs without taking on debt. A liquid account should have three to six months' worth of living expenditures, according to financial experts. Both financial stability and peace of mind are offered by this cushion.

For instance, if your monthly living expenditures come to $3,000, having an emergency fund ranging from $9,000 to $18,000 would help you deal with unanticipated needs like auto or medical repairs.

8) Go Investing Right Away
Because of the power of compounding, time is a crucial component in the generation of

wealth. Your money may increase in value the sooner you begin investing. Over time, even modest, consistent investments may accumulate substantially.

For instance, you might amass more than $150,000 in 20 years if you invest $100 a month in a diversified portfolio with an average yearly return of 7%.

9) Make Your Portfolio Diverse
Investing in a variety of asset types, such as bonds, real estate, and stocks, may help lower risk. Over time, a diversified portfolio may provide more consistent returns by mitigating the effects of market swings.

As an example, you may diversify your investments by holding a combination of stocks, bonds, and real estate investment trusts (REITs) rather than investing all of your money in a single company. The other asset classes could make up for any losses if one does badly.

10) Increase Your Salary
Accelerating your wealth-building path might include side gigs, entrepreneurship, or professional promotion to increase your income. Think about how you can improve your abilities and look into possibilities for better-paying jobs or side gigs.

As an example, you may make additional money for investments or debt repayment by beginning an internet company or taking on freelance work in addition to your full-time employment.

11) Steer clear of schemes
Steer clear of high-risk investments that promise unrealistic returns and get-rich-quick scams. Scammers often take advantage of people's desire for rapid money. Before making any financial commitments, do extensive study and stick to well-established, regulated investing opportunities.

Example: Steer clear of investments that promise 20% monthly guaranteed returns since they are often too good to be true and might cost you money.

12) Examining Financial Textbooks
Increasing your financial literacy is essential to making wise choices. Gaining knowledge about investing, wealth management, and budgeting techniques may be achieved by reading books written by respected financial professionals.

In summary
In summary, making quick money without having any money is an ambitious goal that calls for a strong work ethic, cunning, and inventiveness. These tried-and-true suggestions provide a strong basis for achieving financial success over time, even if there are no quick fixes for obtaining riches right now.

Anybody may pave the route toward a more wealthy future by emphasizing financial knowledge, taking advantage of possibilities for personal development, and persistently saving and investing. Recall that building wealth is a journey, not a sprint, and that the initial step toward financial stability and empowerment is what starts the trip.

www.ingramcontent.com/pod-product-compliance
Lightning Source LLC
Chambersburg PA
CBHW071936210526
45479CB00002B/702